SHIRE NATURAL H

THE HEDGEHOG

P. A. MORRIS

CONTENTS

Cover: *An old male hedgehog showing the coarse, sparse hair on its face and flanks.*

Series editor: Jim Flegg

Copyright © 1988 by P. A. Morris. First published 1988, reprinted 1992.
Number 32 in the Shire Natural History series. ISBN 0 85263 958 9.

Printed in Great Britain by C. I. Thomas & Sons (Haverfordwest) Ltd, Press Buildings, Merlins Bridge, Haverfordwest, Dyfed SA61 1XF.

Introduction and description

The hedgehog is a familiar creature, the only British mammal with a spiny coat. The name 'hedgehog' is relatively new, only a few hundred years old, and is closely related to the many 'country' names, like 'furzehog' and 'hedgepig', inspired by the animal's habit of snuffling about in bushes and hedgerows. The name 'urchin' is also still used sometimes, but the hedgehog's old Anglo-Saxon name was *il*, a contraction of the German name *igel*. Whatever name is used, the hedgehog is universally recognised and it enjoys a popularity (in spite of its prickly coat) which is denied to rats, mice and many other mammals. Yet, despite its familiarity, wide distribution and relative abundance, many aspects of the hedgehog's natural history are still very poorly known.

Hedgehogs all look similar, but they are very variable in detail, leading to considerable controversy over just how many species there really are. There is a single species in Britain and north-west Europe, *Erinaceus europaeus,* with another (*E. algirus*) in North Africa, Spain and the south of France. The eastern European hedgehog is characterised by a white throat and chest, is generally larger and is often considered as a separate species (*E. roumanicus = E. concolor*). There are other hedgehogs in Africa and northern Asia, but none in America or Australasia, though the British hedgehog was introduced to New Zealand in the nineteenth century and is now abundant and widespread there.

The British hedgehog has been described as a separate subspecies (*E. europaeus occidentalis*), on the basis of relatively minor differences. This, however, is unjustified in a species which is so variable.

PHYSICAL DESCRIPTION

It may seem superfluous to describe such a distinctive animal as the hedgehog, but relatively few people have inspected hedgehogs closely, partly because of the difficulty and discomfort of doing so. The animal has five toes on each foot, each furnished with a stout, flattened claw, well suited to digging. The eyes are not large for a nocturnal animal and both ears and tail are present but rather small. Sex determination is easy, provided the animal can be persuaded to uncurl, the male (known as the 'boar') having a prominent penis where one would expect the navel to be.

A hedgehog's skeleton is unspecialised, though both tail and neck are unusually short. The skull is more distinctive. The two front upper teeth are large enough to be mistaken for canines, though they are incisors and have a large and characteristic gap between them. Behind each of these lie two tiny incisors, at the sides of the mouth where one would expect premolars to be. The true canine is the first tooth on the maxilla; it is small and unusual in having two roots. The first lower incisors are also unusual in that they are large and directed forwards as well as upwards. Moreover, they do not bite against their counterparts in the upper jaw, but into that large gap between them. The premolars have sharp cusps well suited to crunching up a diversity of foods. The deciduous dentition, consisting of 24 milk teeth, is replaced within a few weeks of birth. The dentitions of hedgehogs are unusually variable and 10 per cent or more may have dental or skull anomalies. Despite the possession of 36 teeth in the full set, hedgehogs will rarely bite humans, even if provoked.

THE SPINES

The hedgehog's most obvious feature is its spines. These do not cover the whole body: the belly, tail, legs and face are clothed instead with sparse, coarse grey-brown hair. Although other mammals (for example, porcupines, echidnas and spiny mice) have spines, those of the hedgehog are more elaborate than in any other species. As Aristotle observed, each spine consists of a modified hair. It is sharply pointed, with a broad dark brown band towards the tip; the rest of the shaft is a creamy colour. Where the spine enters the hedgehog's skin it narrows to form a 'neck' and bends through

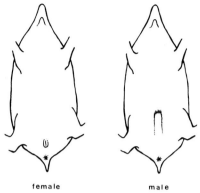

female   male

1. Male and female hedgehogs are easily told apart — if they can be persuaded to uncurl and show their undersides.

about 60 degrees. Within the skin it terminates in a bulbous knob, which prevents spines being pulled out.

Attached to the bulb are the tiny muscles which erect the spine. At rest, these muscles are relaxed and the spines lie flat, like the fur of a dog. However, when disturbed, the hedgehog can erect some or all of its spines, each pointing in a different direction, presenting a bristling mass to an attacker. The skin musculature has further elaborations which allow the hedgehog to retract its legs, pull in its head and tail and draw the spiny skin under the body to cover the soft underbelly. A circular muscle lying in the skin (the *orbicularis*), at the junction of the spiny and hairy regions, can then contract like the drawstring of a kit-bag. The hedgehog becomes entirely enclosed by the spiny skin and can thus roll into a ball, completely protected by prickles on all sides. Moreover, if the animal is hit, or falls from a height, the spines bend at their 'necks' to absorb the blow and are not driven back into the skin.

Young hedgehogs usually have spines which are crisply marked in black and white, whereas in older animals the spines tend to be shades of cream and brown, though this is not an infallible guide to age. Albino hedgehogs are occasionally reported and partial albinos are not uncommon. All-black (melanic) individuals have never been recorded. Hedgehogs completely lacking spines

have been reported. One was exhibited, stuffed, at a scientific meeting in 1898 but was probably a hoax. In the twentieth century, a live hedgehog kept as a pet in Bedfordshire, and otherwise apparently in good health, lost all its spines as it grew up. It is not clear whether this was a genetic defect or due to some misfortune, but in the wild such a defenceless animal would not survive very long.

A hedgehog has about 3500 spines when it is weaned; more are added as it grows and adults have about 7000. There is no regular moult, as in other mammals; spines are lost and replaced haphazardly just like human hair. Any one spine may persist in the skin for up to eighteen months.

BODY WEIGHT

Apart from its spines, the hedgehog has no remarkable features visible externally, except a considerable variation in body size. Juveniles weigh from 120 grams (4 ounces), when they leave the nest, to more than 500 grams (1 pound 2 ounces) later in the season. Adults can weigh less than 400 grams (14 ounces) at the end of winter, to over 1500 grams (3 pounds 5 ounces), in the case of some particularly large males. An individual's weight varies seasonally by 300 grams (11 ounces) or more due to the accumulation and consumption of fat reserves for hibernation. Generally boars are larger than sows, but the average difference between them is less than the seasonal variation of individuals. In captivity,

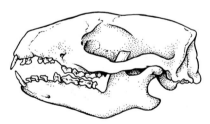

2. The adult hedgehog's skull is about 50 mm (2 inches) long. The dentition consists of sharply pointed teeth which are usually somewhat smoothed by wear. The two front upper incisors resemble canines and the two front lower incisors bite into the gap between them. No other mammal has such an arrangement.

3

some individuals can become very large, weighing over 2 kg (4½ pounds). European hedgehogs, though the same species, are often bigger than British ones.

SIGNS

For most people, the commonest encounter with hedgehogs is that of finding their pathetic remains squashed on the roads during the summer. Their tracks are much less likely to be found and they do not leave characteristic food remains. However, their droppings are quite distinctive: dark grey or black, 2 to 3 cm (¾ to 1¼ inches) long, only 1 cm (½ inch) in diameter and characteristically studded with the glossy fragments of chewed-up beetles. These are a common sight on garden lawns and are often the first indication of nocturnal visits by hedgehogs.

DISTRIBUTION

The hedgehog occurs over most of the lowlands of western Europe, in places up to 2000 metres (6500 feet) above sea level. Its southern limit is the Mediterranean coast (though it is found on some Mediterranean islands, probably as a result of introduction). In the north it does not extend far beyond latitude 60 degrees north (southern Scandinavia). Hedgehogs are thus found in a wide variety of climates and habitats.

The hedgehog is found throughout mainland Britain, though it is scarce or absent in areas of mountain, moorland and marsh. It is particularly abundant in farmland and hedgerows and it is one of the few mammals that seem to thrive in urban habitats, such as parks and gardens, deep in the heart of cities. For example, there are permanent hedgehog populations in some of the central London parks and they are abundant in the inner suburbs. A London hedgehog once penetrated Britain's security system and was found inside the Admiralty building in Whitehall.

Unlike many mammals, hedgehogs are found in Ireland and also on many of the offshore islands of Britain. Few of these can have been colonised naturally; introduction is far more likely. Hedgehogs need not have been introduced deliberately because they are very prone to being accidentally scooped up with loads of thatching, peat or animal fodder and may have been widely transported among such materials in prehistoric times. Hedgehogs have been taken to North Ronaldsay, where they have prospered, perhaps at the expense of nesting sea birds. Introductions have also been attempted to certain other islands, though this should not be encouraged.

3. *Hedgehogs occur widely in Britain and Ireland but tend to be scarce or absent in upland areas and certain other habitats. They are found on many islands, usually as a result of introduction in the past.*

Behaviour

Though normally considered an unathletic creature, akin to a clockwork toy, a hedgehog can run faster than a man can walk. Hedgehogs can also swim yet, perversely, they are often drowned in swimming pools and the smallest of garden ponds, mainly because they cannot get out and soon become exhausted. Contrary to belief, hedgehogs do climb readily; they have been known to hiber-

4. *Hedgehogs have five fingers and five toes, each with strong but blunt claws, useful for digging.*

5. *Often the first indication of hedgehogs in the garden is the appearance of characteristic dark droppings on the lawn, about 50 mm (2 inches) long, crinkly and studded with undigested food remains.*

nate in thatched roofs and climb into upstairs bedrooms. Hedgehogs also dig, and in the colder parts of Europe they may even excavate their own burrows for hibernation.

As the hedgehog is nocturnal and not easy to observe for long periods, very little is known about its social and other behaviour. However, 'courtship' behaviour is commonly witnessed, especially in early summer: the male continually circling a female, whilst loud snorting noises are produced by one or both partners.

Hedgehogs occasionally fight vigorously, one animal attempting to butt another and bowl it over. There is no evidence that they are territorial, yet fights among both wild and captive animals show that hedgehogs are not wholly tolerant of each other. Studies in captivity suggest that fighting establishes a 'pecking order' of social seniority, yet several different hedgehogs may be observed to visit the same place, even simultaneously, suggesting that they do not hold mutually exclusive territories in the wild, in the way that some birds do, and are willing to tolerate at least some of their neighbours.

A hedgehog's eyesight is not particularly well developed and its eyes are very close to the ground, limiting the potential use of vision in social behaviour. Its hearing is acute, but hedgehogs are normally silent (except for sundry snorts and snuffles and a rarely heard pig-like squeal occasioned by severe fright), so the possibilities for vocal communication seem limited. The sense of smell is highly developed and extensively used during feeding, so it is possible that scent marking may play a part in social behaviour, but there is no real evidence for this.

Though primarily nocturnal, hedgehogs may be seen during the day, especially in late autumn when young animals are seeking extra food to convert into fat reserves. Sickly animals also frequently become indifferent to daylight.

The most extraordinary piece of hedgehog behaviour is termed 'self-anointing'. Certain individuals are apparently stimulated by astringent substances (leather, varnish, cigar butts and toad skin, among others) to produce large quantities of frothy saliva. This they throw back on to their body and spines, by extending the tongue and twisting the body to an extraordinary degree. This remarkably energetic and messy performance can continue for twenty minutes, until the body appears to be coated with soap suds. Then the behaviour abruptly ceases and the hedgehog resumes its normal business.

Self-anointing seems to occupy the animal's total attention at the time, yet its function is obscure. It is not part of the normal grooming behaviour, nor is there any evident effect on the resident flea population. Various other explanatory theories have been aired, the most plausible being that the spines become coated with a mild poison which enhances their protective function. However, anyone who handles hedgehogs will know that the spines are an effective and uncomfortable deterrent anyway: there is no need for any salivary embellishment!

Self-anointing has been filmed and photographed. It is an established, if enigmatic, part of the hedgehog's behaviour, but what of the numerous stories about hedgehogs carrying fruit (usually apples) on their spines? These tales are centuries old, being depicted, for example, in a thirteenth-century illustrated manuscript, yet there is no hard evidence that they are true nor any obvious explanation for such behaviour. Why should a hedgehog carry away fruit when it does not store food, and why concern itself with fruit anyway when its principal diet is invertebrates? It would, however, be unwise to dismiss these stories as fabrications, if only because of their persistence.

The same applies to the uncorroborated accounts of hedgehogs taking milk from cows. There are no photographs (except of udder damage) and plenty of reasons for doubt, yet, to many country people, suckling cows is a perfectly accepted part of normal hedgehog activity. Could a hedgehog reach a cow's udder? Could it open its mouth wide enough to suckle and, if so, would the cow tolerate a hedgehog's sharp teeth? These may all seem unlikely, but is it any more probable that a story which is so firmly entrenched has no factual basis at all?

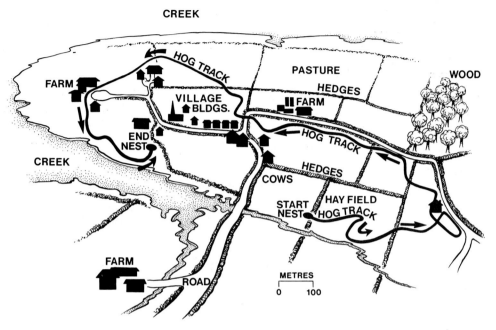

6. *A night's wanderings, based upon a male hedgehog that was followed all night in his search for females and food (probably in that order of priority). He left his nest in a hedge, headed east to a garden, then west across pastureland and through the village, finally going to bed at dawn in a small patch of weeds having covered more than 3 km (2 miles).*

Home range and movements

Field studies based upon systematic trapping have revealed much about the lives of small mammals like mice and voles, but hedgehogs are too few and too large for the convenient application of standard small-mammal study methods. On the other hand, hedgehogs are too small and secretive to be easily watched like badgers or deer.

It is here that an amateur mammalogist may make a useful contribution to our knowledge of hedgehogs, using a simple mark-recapture scheme to investigate hedgehog movements. Hedgehogs may be marked by painting patches of spines different colours or painting large numbers on them. Such marks persist for several weeks at least but may be worn off or obscured by dirt within a few months. Better marks are made by clipping patches of spines in individually recognisable combinations (for example, right shoulder and left hip, or left shoulder and middle back). This does not hurt the animal as spines, like hairs, are not living material. Such marks remain easily visible for over a year, except in young animals where the growth of extra spines may obscure the mark somewhat sooner.

7

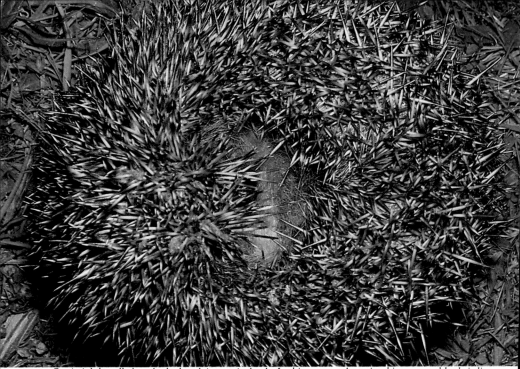

7. *A tightly rolled-up hedgehog lying on its back. In this posture the animal is protected by bristling spines on all sides. Adults are almost impossible for predators to defeat, though weaker young hedgehogs may be successfully bitten or torn apart by badgers or the larger species of owl.*

8. *The X-ray of a rolled-up hedgehog shows how closely the head is tucked round in between the feet. During hibernation the animal may spend several weeks in this posture.*

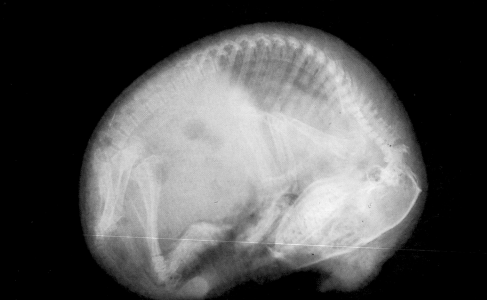

9. *A true albino in which no pigment is present in the spines or on the nose and feet. The eyes are also without pigment and appear pink.*

10. *'Alice', the naked hedgehog of Luton, began life with a set of sparse spines but lost them all. The reason for this is not clear but may have been a genetic anomaly. She was saved from being killed by predators and lived for several years as a pet.*

People have marked their regular visiting hedgehog, only to find that 'it' turns out to be a dozen or more animals which may be using their garden at different times, and some may appear in another place 200 to 300 metres (220 to 330 yards) away, even on the same evening. Despite their simplicity, few of these mark-recapture studies have been carried out systematically for any length of time. However, they usually involve a low recapture rate: a few individuals remain in the same area for at least several days or weeks, but many are never seen again. This suggests that some hedgehogs may be permanent wanderers, that hedgehogs in general are very wide-ranging creatures, or maybe that the nomads are mainly youngsters looking for an unoccupied area in which to live. There is much to be learned from careful fieldwork regarding these matters. Marking individuals which regularly visit a food bowl also permits the study of social behaviour (for example, are males dominant over females or big animals over small?).

Radio tracking has been used to investigate hedgehog ecology in more detail. A small radio transmitter fixed to a hedgehog's spines broadcasts the animal's position day and night until the batteries are exhausted. A direction-finding receiver detects the signal and may be used to locate the animal at any time without disturbing it. This reveals that hedgehogs may use different areas at different times of year, and that they do not wander at random but have a good idea of the geography of their surroundings. One animal found its nest, over 300 metres (330 yards) away, in less than an hour and returned a similar distance to its feeding area the same night. How did it know the way?

Radio tracking reveals that male hedgehogs consistently travel further and faster than females, up to 3 km (2 miles) in a night. A male's home range can cover 30 ha (74 acres) or more, encompassing the ranges of several females. In order to cover so much ground, the males often do not return to the nest where they spent the previous day. They seem to change their daytime nest very frequently, whereas females (even when they do not have young) continue to use the same nest for a week or ten days at a stretch. There is a strong possibility that home-range sizes vary with habitat, hedgehogs in woodland areas moving about less than those inhabiting more open places like fields and parkland.

Food

The hedgehog is mainly carnivorous but will eat almost anything edible that it can reach. The diet varies considerably with season and habitat, but beetles (particularly carabids) are the most frequent prey, though earthworms, caterpillars and other insect larvae are important food, as are slugs and earwigs, making the hedgehog an ally of the gardener. Curiously, woodlice and snails are relatively rarely eaten, despite their abundance in most usual hedgehog haunts. Hedgehogs will readily take carrion and also devour millipedes and species of beetle which produce unpleasant secretions as a protection against predators. That a hedgehog will consume these distasteful items suggests an undiscriminating palate, yet in captivity hedgehogs exercise distinct food preferences when given a choice. The abundance of the larger invertebrates at night probably accounts for the hedgehog being a nocturnal species. Its spines would appear to provide adequate protection for it to be diurnal, but its invertebrate prey is much more difficult to find during the hours of daylight.

Hedgehogs have been credited with regularly killing and eating snakes. They do eat snakes, though they are not a significant part of their diet; hedgehog blood has a degree of immunity to adder venom. In addition, the snake striking against a hedgehog's sharp spines would damage itself severely and expend its venom, often without achieving a puncture of the skin. Once exhausted, the snake would be easy prey, though snakes are not normally active at night when the hedgehogs are out foraging. Hedgehogs also eat other reptiles and amphibians but lizards and frogs are more likely to be

11. Hedgehogs probably do not tackle adders as often as folklore suggests but are nevertheless well protected by their spines and they also have a special immunity to snake venom.

consumed as carrion than to be chased and killed.

Hedgehogs will also chase and kill mammals such as mice; even live rabbits have been reported as victims. It is therefore not surprising that the chicks of ground-nesting birds (for example, pipits and larks) may be preyed upon and hedgehogs can do considerable damage in gull and tern colonies (though far less than foxes or crows). Economically important birds such as partridges and pheasants are also at risk. The hedgehog is not blameless here and gamekeepers have consequently persecuted them as vermin for centuries. However, careful studies of the fate of several thousand partridge nests have revealed that hedgehogs probably take less than 5 per cent of the eggs, considerably fewer than are accidentally destroyed by farm machinery. Similarly, pheasant nests are also raided by hedgehogs, but no more than by dogs and cats and far less than by foxes and crows.

Part of hedgehogs' success in urban areas is probably due to the extra food put out for them by householders. Plates of bread and milk are eagerly devoured and provide a source of liquid in dry weather (when worms and other natural food are hard to find). Extra food like this is also vital in the autumn to help underweight young animals build up sufficient fat reserves to last the winter. Wild hedgehogs will travel 500 metres (550 yards) or more to visit a favourite food bowl but do not necessarily then choose to nest nearby in the same garden. Nor do they become harmfully addicted to artificial food but treat it as a welcome supplement to their natural diet.

However, much as they may like bread and milk, it is unwise to feed captive hedgehogs only on this diet as it gives them diarrhoea. This is because cow's milk has a component which is indigestible and upsets the hedgehog's intestines. This is particularly damaging to baby hedgehogs and not helpful to sickly animals either, so cow's milk should not be given to them in captivity. Goat's milk seems harmless and also milk substitute baby foods. Wild hedgehogs can cope because they eat many other things in addition, but even here it is wise to dilute the cow's milk with water. A better diet would be a varied mixture of table scraps or tinned dog food (though not fish-based cat foods).

12. *Hedgehogs have surprisingly long legs and can climb quite well.*

13. *Hedgehogs can swim quite well but frequently drown in small garden ponds because they cannot climb out.*

14. *Hedgehog 'courtship' is a noisy affair. Both partners snort loudly as the male circles the female and she flinches or bunches her spines to repel his advances.*

15. *Self-anointing is a peculiar activity in which the hedgehog twists its body into extraordinary positions to deposit frothy saliva over its spines.*

Hibernation and the yearly cycle

The hedgehog is a true hibernator, unlike squirrels, badgers and other animals which merely become inactive for short periods during inclement winter weather. Contrary to popular belief, hedgehogs do not suddenly begin hibernating at a given time then remain solidly 'asleep' until a particular date in the spring. Cool nights and shortage of food in the autumn cause the animals to become less and less active, though a warm period (or regular provision of food) may revive and extend normal activity well into November and December. There are thus no fixed hibernation dates, though the general level of activity probably declines earlier in cooler regions and hedgehogs in Scotland may hibernate for three or four weeks longer than those in the south of England. Males seem to hibernate earlier than females. Some hedgehogs continue to be active as late as Christmas, but these are likely to be young animals still striving to build up sufficient fat reserves to last the winter.

Even during the coldest months of January and February, some animals may be active for short periods. Experiments in controlled laboratory conditions suggest that hibernating hedgehogs wake up naturally with a remarkable regularity every ten days or so, even when kept undisturbed in constant temperatures. Therefore, again contrary to popular belief, hibernation is not an unbroken event. In the wild, hedgehogs can awake and build a new winter nest at any time; very few remain in the same nest for the whole winter.

It is vital that the hedgehog has an adequate food store to last through the winter but, whereas hibernating rodents often prepare caches of nuts and seeds, hedgehogs store their food internally in the form of fat. Masses of white fat are deposited below the skin and among the viscera, especially in early autumn.

Steady consumption of these reserves over winter causes a loss of up to one third of the total body weight.

The hedgehog also needs large stores of brown fat. Unlike white fat, which is widely distributed about the body, brown fat forms discrete orange-brown lobes around the neck and shoulders. This is a special tissue whose role is to generate heat when the body temperature needs to be raised to the normal level. An adequate store of brown fat is thus essential if the animal is to arouse from the 'cold-blooded' state of hibernation. Before their true function was known, these fat lobes were at one time called 'hibernating glands', because of their prominence in hibernators, especially during the autumn.

The hedgehog has been extensively used as an experimental animal in laboratory investigations of the anatomical and physiological changes that occur during hibernation. It is found that the heart slows from over one hundred and fifty beats to less than twenty per minute and is apparently specially modified so that it can function at low temperatures and not undergo fibrillation, as happens with other mammal hearts when they are cooled below normal blood temperatures. Breathing is reduced to about ten irregular breaths per minute. Considerable changes occur in the structure of various organs and there are significant changes in the blood. The body temperature falls from 34 C (93 F) to match that of the environment (though it is never allowed to drop below freezing point). The much reduced metabolic activity ensures that fat reserves will fuel the body for longer than if a higher level of activity were maintained.

Hibernation is thus an important stratagem for survival during the winter months when food is scarce. All these factors demonstrate that hibernation is a major physiological readjustment, not just a deep sleep. A further difference is that sleep is a biological necessity, while hibernation is optional. Hedgehogs kept warm and well fed indoors do not hibernate, but they still have to sleep in the normal way. During the winter, it is essential for hedgehogs to be kept cool in order to hibernate successfully and use their fat reserves efficiently. Many people try to be kind to hedgehogs in cold weather by keeping them warm, but this can be harmful unless they are kept warm enough, that is, over about 15 to 20 C (59 to 68 F), to remain fully active. The best temperature is about 5 C (41 F).

THE WINTER NEST

Despite the impressive volume of detailed information about hibernation in laboratory conditions, little is known about what wild hedgehogs do in winter. The winter nest (the 'hibernaculum') is all-important. This provides the hedgehog's sole protection against the worst weather of the year. The nest is carefully constructed, usually under some suitable supporting structure like a pile of brushwood, a low bramble bush or a garden shed. Hedgehogs may also occupy rabbit burrows. Dry leaves are collected at n.ght, pushed into a pile and then the animal enters the heap and shuffles around inside. The leaves become tightly packed to form a weatherproof layer, 10 cm (4 inches) thick or more, surrounding the hedgehog. Several of these nests may be built and abandoned before one is chosen for use and occupied for up to six months, though occupancy normally lasts only a few weeks before another nest is built. The leafy walls of the nest provide very effective insulation, protecting the occupant against extreme cold and also insulating the hedgehog from brief warm periods which might cause it to awake unnecessarily. The nest walls resist decay and can last for over a year, though, once abandoned after a brief period of use, a hibernaculum is unlikely to be reoccupied. Hedgehogs normally hibernate alone, though often several will have their hibernacula relatively close together in some particularly favourable site, suggesting again that they are not strictly territorial creatures.

It is likely that many garden hedgehogs find difficulty locating a suitable place to nest for the winter. Many gardens are too small and too tidy to offer appropriate sites and nesting materials. Piles of brushwood, hedge cuttings and similar are very attractive nesting sites and many hedgehogs are probably incinerated as gardeners burn their refuse without first turning it over to check for hedgehog inhabitants.

Although grass, bracken and other materials may be incorporated into the hibernaculum, these are probably less weatherproof than a mass of tightly packed leaves. The crucial importance of leaves for the construction of vital winter nests may be one of the most important factors governing the hedgehog's ecology. An omnivorous animal is unlikely to be limited by the distribution of food, but the need for broad-leafed trees may be a reason why hedgehogs are rare or absent (as mentioned earlier) in habitats such as mountains and moorland where deciduous trees and suitable hibernaculum sites are few. Moreover, across Europe, the hedgehog's northern limit of distribution is about 60 degrees latitude, the approximate limit of deciduous trees. In Finland, hedgehogs do occur further north, but usually only in gardens and man-made habitats where substitute nesting sites and materials are available.

Elaborate nests are less important during the summer months, though females construct a large home for their family. Apart from these 'nursery nests', hedgehogs often do not trouble to build much of a shelter if the weather is warm; they merely lie up in suitably thick vegetation or under a bush. They will even nest beside noisy roads where sleep appears impossible.

Breeding

Male hedgehogs are capable of breeding from April until August, which means that their reproductive organs must develop very rapidly from the shrunken, quiescent state in which they are found during the winter. Within a month of coming out of hibernation a male hedgehog's accessory reproductive organs have grown enormously, often exceeding 5 per cent of the total body weight. This rapid and extreme enlargement (particularly of the seminal vesicles, prostate and Cowper's glands) is probably unrivalled by any other mammal and yet has no obvious functional explanation.

Mating is rarely witnessed, and there is

16. *Radio tracking allows us to follow hedgehogs and find out where they go. The animal has a small transmitter glued to its spines and can be located from up to 500 metres (550 yards) away using the direction-finding aerial. Our present understanding of hedgehog movements owes much to the patient work of student helpers.*

17. *Traditionally people put out bread and milk for hedgehogs, which may travel over 500 metres (550 yards) to get it. However, a more varied diet would be better and the milk should always be diluted with water. Captives should not be fed bread and milk as it causes diarrhoea.*

18. *Baby hedgehogs quickly grow a set of about a hundred white spines. After a few days brown spines begin to grow among them. The eyes do not open until later.*

19. *When they leave the maternal nest at about five weeks old, young hedgehogs are very vulnerable. During the summer they can probably look after themselves, but during the cold nights of autumn they can be usefully rescued and fed on milk substitutes (not cow's milk) and later dog food. They are more likely to survive once they weigh over 500 grams (18 ounces).*

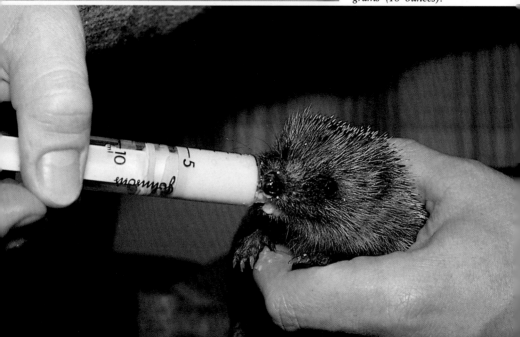

considerable popular speculation about how the act is accomplished by such prickly partners. The female can lay her spines down so that they do not impale her mate. She also stretches her body flat out and extends her hindquarters to be more accessible. Whatever the difficulties, they are not insuperable and females are found pregnant from May until October. The gestation period is about 34 days but can vary in length by four or five days. This is unusual, for most mammals appear to have a fairly fixed duration for their pregnancies. A possible explanation is that pregnancies (especially early ones) may be interrupted by a few days of cold weather, causing the female to become torpid. This could slow foetal development and thus prolong gestation. A similar phenomenon has been demonstrated in pipistrelle bats (which, like the hedgehog, also may be pregnant before shaking off the last remnants of hibernation), but this has not yet been proved to occur in the hedgehog.

The average litter size is between four and five, though some females produce only two young, others up to seven. The babies are born blind, pink and helpless. Many books suggest that the young are born with white spines which later turn brown. However, there are no spines visible at birth; they would pose a serious threat to the mother, even if they were soft. Instead, the skin is swollen and covers the spines, but soon after birth it shrinks and the spines are rapidly revealed. These first spines are white and there are about one hundred of them. A day or two later the first typical brown spines appear, growing up among the white spines which may persist (but never go brown) for several months. More brown spines grow up to supplement those already present, until there are two thousand or more.

The babies can partially roll up at eleven days old and their eyes open at fourteen days. When they are about three weeks old, the mother leads her family out of the nest each night in a foraging procession. The young thus learn to feed for themselves and become independent of the mother and her milk at about four to six weeks of age. The family then gradually disperses to lead solitary lives.

The male takes no part in rearing the family.

Whereas in rabbits (for example) there is a high embryo mortality, in the hedgehog most of the young conceived survive to birth. However, if a mother is disturbed within a day or two of giving birth, she will eat her young. Later, when they have grown a little more, disturbance will cause her to move the whole family one at a time to a new nest. Each baby is carried in her teeth by the scruff of the neck. It seems that rearing a large litter is not easy and about 20 per cent of all hedgehogs that are born do not survive the first month of life. An average litter may thus lose one baby; larger families suffer a greater loss and the mother finally rears successfully an average of about three offspring.

Females are sometimes found pregnant in September and it is likely that these late litters are mostly second families, the females having already raised one that year. If early litters are lost, females may even have a third litter, at least in captivity. However, it has not been proved that females do have two litters in a year in the wild; it may be that the late families are produced by females who were too young to breed at the normal time in May and June. These late litters will be born into an increasingly hostile environment. It may be late October before they leave the nest, and they stand little chance of finding much food unless the arrival of harsh winter weather is considerably delayed. At the very time they most need food to grow and to lay down fat reserves for support during hibernation, they are least able to find worms, beetles and other prey. Consequently, undersized young hedgehogs are often found foraging during the autumn, even in daylight, and as late as Christmas Day. It appears that a minimum weight of at least 450 grams (1 pound) is necessary to survive hibernation; animals smaller than this have insufficient fat to last until the following season. Thus, any of these small hedgehogs found in the autumn stand little chance of survival if left to their own devices. If they are taken into captivity and fed well for a few weeks, they can then be released with a greatly enhanced life expectancy.

20. *Mating is a delicate business in which the female arches her back downwards, causing the spines to bunch up around her head in a peculiar way.*

Hedgehogs do not breed in the year of their birth, but those that survive their first winter are ready to breed when they are about one year old. They can then continue to breed at least into their sixth year.

Survival and predation

Investigation of survival and longevity requires some method of age determination. While some animals appear to be old or are obviously very big, it is impossible to be certain that they are old. There are no reliable external signs of age, so such studies must usually be based upon laboratory investigation of dead animals. Some zoologists have found that tooth wear provides a clue as to whether one animal is older than another, but in hedgehogs, with such a varied diet, the rate at which their teeth are worn away must depend more on what they have been eating than upon how old they are.

A better age determination method uses thin, stained sections of the lower jaw. Under a microscope 'growth rings' are visible in the bone. These are just like the annual rings of trees and reflect the interruptions of bone growth caused during hibernation. The number of lines is thus a record of the number of winters the animal has lived through. Examination of large samples of hedgehogs provides an insight into the age structure of the population. By comparing the number of animals which are, say, two, three and four years old, it is possible to estimate the survival rates from one year to the next. A comparison of samples of hedgehogs taken in autumn and spring will enable an estimate to be made of the mortality of juveniles during their all-important first winter.

Over half the hedgehogs born never see their first birthday; the late litters are particularly doomed to an early death. Even those born early, with the whole summer to feed and prepare for the winter, face a severe challenge. As pointed out earlier, hibernation is a major physiological stress, quite apart from the fact that a hibernating hedgehog is practically defenceless against floods, melting snow and destruction of its hibernaculum.

Those that do survive their first hibernation stand a fair chance of living a further two or three years. However,

21. *A blood-sucking tick among the spines. Hedgehogs may carry several of these parasites, which drop off when gorged with blood. They may be removed with forceps or, better, made to release their hold by smearing the globular body with detergent or olive oil.*

22. *Rolling up is no defence against approaching motor vehicles and it has been suggested that hedgehogs would increase their chances of survival if they ran away instead.*

every winter is a fresh hazard and only about 30 per cent of adult hedgehogs survive from one year to the next. For the hedgehog 'old age' is about five years and it is probable that only about four animals in a thousand exceed seven years old. The maximum age is likely to be about ten years.

With no adequate population census methods it is difficult to assess the importance of many ecological factors in the hedgehog's life. It is clear that hibernation is a severe test but predation is probably much less significant than in most mammals: the hedgehog's spiny armour is very effective protection. Foxes and badgers take a few, particularly juveniles which cannot roll up tightly, and hedgehogs are among the occasional victims of tawny owls and pine martens. Some gamekeepers still kill hedgehogs in defence of gamebird eggs and chicks and may maintain a high predation rate for many years without exterminating the hedgehog. On one estate in East Anglia, twenty thousand hedgehogs were killed in fifty years with no indication of imminent extinction. Similarly, highway mortality takes a continuous toll with little sign that hedgehog populations are shrinking as a result. Those who condemn gamekeepers and view road casualties as a major threat to hedgehogs might also regard the carnage not as a sign of impending extinction but as evidence of just how abundant and successful the animal is to withstand such unrelenting pressures.

Judging by the numbers of badly injured hedgehogs found in the summer, mowing machines are another modern hazard. Increasingly, farmers cut their grass for silage, together with any hedgehogs that happen to be in the field that day. Local authorities mow road verges to keep weeds under control and reduce fire risks but at the same time are destroying hedgehogs and the sort of places where they spend their summer days. Modern 'strimmer'-type mowing machines are designed to gain access to odd corners and destroy lank vegetation, the very places where mother hedgehogs have their nursery nests. Hedgehogs sustain serious wounds as a result and many more must be killed outright but are

unconsidered because they are out of sight and their demise is less obvious than those squashed on the roads.

It has been suggested that hedgehogs may learn that rolling up is no defence against motor cars and they are more likely to survive by running away. It is argued that those that run survive, but those that roll up are killed. Thus, in a classical example of Darwinian evolution, 'survival of the fittest' will ensure that hedgehogs are increasingly adopting the new habit as an adaptation to modern conditions. The theory is attractively simple but nobody has published statistical evidence showing that hedgehogs now run away more often than they roll up; even this would not constitute proof of the theory because nobody carried out comparative studies before the advent of the motor car. The whole idea may be based on a false assumption: that running away will mean escape from death. Clearly a hedgehog cannot outpace a car by running ahead of it, and running to either side may increase the risk of going under the wheels; by staying still it might be straddled and escape.

FARMING AND GARDENING METHODS

The greatest threats to long-term hedgehog survival and abundance are more insidious and far more serious, made worse by not being so visible. The problem lies with changing farming methods. Pastureland, so good for hedgehogs to forage in, being rich in worms and insects, has been turned into fields for grain and other crops. Arable farmland is treated with chemicals specifically to kill the very species that hedgehogs need for food. Some of the pesticides are persistent and are accumulated by predators from tiny quantities in their prey. Hedgehogs eating contaminated beetles, for example, could build up significant levels of harmful organochlorine residues in their bodies, perhaps leading to sterility or death, as happens in other animals. These chemicals accumulate in fat, and because fat is so important to hedgehogs (in hibernation) they might be especially vulnerable. However, nobody has carried out any research into this problem, partly because of the cost.

21

Even without harmful chemicals, hedgehogs still face a major problem on modern farms. Whereas old pasture offers food and shelter (in clumps of weeds or odd corners), arable land is ploughed up every year, harvested and then lies bare and open until the new crop grows. This is hardly a secure or supportive hedgehog habitat. The increase in the size of fields and the reduction in the number of hedgerows also make life more difficult and, since these changes in farming practice extend over such large areas of countryside, hedgehogs must now be far less abundant than previously.

Farmers are not the only users of dangerous chemicals. Gardeners, often well meaning hedgehog lovers, also use pesticides with similar potential dangers in great quantities. If a danger to hedgehogs is perceived at all, it usually centres on the role of slug pellets. These are dangerous to pets and children (as well as to hedgehogs) and should never be left in heaps where many could be eaten at once. To lessen this risk, the pellets are generally hard, dry, distasteful and coloured blue, all intended to reduce their attractiveness to mammals and garden birds. However, there is the problem that hedgehogs might eat slugs that had already been poisoned and thus poison themselves. Studies reveal that this is not a very serious danger as long as the pellets only contain metaldehyde, but increasingly they seem to have other poisonous ingredients whose effects on hedgehogs have not been assessed.

Even more important is the fact that there are many garden pesticides at least as dangerous as slug pellets but, being liquids, they are not so visible and soon forgotten. They are often used as sprays but long grass sprayed with certain weed-killers during the day is a dangerous place for hedgehogs to forage at night. Sprays are often not used on the ground where hedgehogs will come into contact with them. Nevertheless, they are still washed off by rain and into the soil, there to contaminate the hedgehog's food (and that of garden birds, amphibians and other desirable wildlife).

Parasites and disease

The hedgehog has a reputation for being flea-ridden: there may be up to five hundred on a single animal (though usually only a dozen or so). These fleas (*Archaeopsylla erinacei*) are highly host-specific (and very visible among the spines) and are rarely found on other animals. They can transfer to humans and pets but are not comfortable on their new host and are unlikely to remain. Hedgehogs are unjustly blamed for the fleas on cats and dogs; these have their own different but closely related species. Moreover, the hedgehog itself is a rather special host, and so few other types of flea will live on it.

The hedgehogs that were introduced to New Zealand lost their fleas somewhere on the voyage from Europe. In their absence certain mites have become the major hedgehog ectoparasite (and evidently cause many deaths). Mites are not common on British hedgehogs and seem to do little harm to them. Sometimes crusty scabs are caused by mite infestations but these respond readily to acaricide preparations from veterinary surgeons and pet shops.

Hedgehogs are often found carrying large, shiny grey ticks (usually *Ixodes hexagonus*). Up to fifty of their globular bodies may be counted on one host, but they do not usually remain long and drop off after feeding on their host's blood. The hedgehog seems remarkably indifferent towards such parasites and makes little effort to rid itself of them. Ticks can be encouraged to depart by smearing their round bodies with olive oil or glycerine (which blocks their breathing holes, causing suffocation).

Hedgehogs also carry a special type of ringworm fungus: about one in five is infected. Males are more often affected than females, urban hedgehogs more often than rural ones (possibly because the latter live at lower densities). The fungus does little noticeable harm and there is often no visible sign of it. Some old animals with chronic infections have dry, swollen ears and should be handled with caution because the ringworm can be transmitted to humans. However, this does not seem to happen often, nor does it cause a serious problem.

Many hedgehogs become infected with lungworms (small nematodes). In severe cases the host develops a form of bronchitis and makes audible gurgling noises while breathing. The worms also damage the lungs and in Europe are considered to be a serious cause of hedgehog mortality. Treatment with sheep lungworm medicine can be effective.

The only economically serious pathogen that hedgehogs carry is cattle foot and mouth disease. They are surprisingly resistant to this and, if infected before hibernation, will still be capable of spreading the disease months later when they become active again. Potentially the hedgehog could thus reinfect a 'clean' herd, but nobody has demonstrated that hedgehogs do play a significant role in the spread of foot and mouth. Nor has anyone shown that hedgehogs carry rabies, even in Europe where it is established in other forms of wildlife. So, in the unfortunate event of the disease being introduced to Britain, the hedgehog's role in spreading it is not likely to be very significant.

Hedgehogs and man

In 1566 Queen Elizabeth I signed into law an 'Acte for pr'servacon of grayne' in which hedgehogs were included among the 'noxious birds and vermin' whose destruction was to be encouraged by churchwardens paying a bounty for each one killed in their parish. The Act was repealed in 1863, but for three hundred years hedgehogs were a statutory pest. Old churchwardens' accounts still exist showing payments made for decades, usually two or three pence per snout or tail. These bounties must have been useful pocket money for the local people but can have done little to preserve grain or anything else.

Hedgehogs are not without sin, but the effort that goes into trapping them as 'vermin' is probably not cost-effective in terms of damage prevented, and the practice would probably cease but for the fact that the same traps kill other more serious villains such as stoats and brown rats. The hedgehog's principal food consists of those invertebrates which are considerable agricultural and horticultural pests. Thus, on balance, the hedgehog's feeding behaviour is probably more beneficial than harmful, and in suburban gardens this is certainly so.

Hedgehogs have been used for many minor purposes: their dried skins were utilised for combing out sheep fleeces ('carding') before spinning; the spines make good pins for use in situations where metal pins would corrode; and gypsies used to bake them in clay for a tasty snack. Scientifically, the hedgehog is seen as one of the most primitive of living mammals and a study of its brain, teeth, skull and other important zoological features helps to interpret what we know from fossils about the evolution of animals that lived long ago. The hedgehog has also been used as an experimental tool for investigating the physiology of hibernation. This phenomenon is of interest in itself, but the knowledge gained has been applied to the development of techniques for cooling the body during major surgery. Studies are also in progress aimed at finding out how the hedgehog's heart continues to function at low temperatures; this too may one day be useful in treating human heart problems.

Hedgehogs are popular story-book animals, despite being less cuddlesome than almost anything else! They also make endearing pets and will soon become tame. Some even learn to respond to a name. They are easy to keep, though often somewhat smelly. However, they are not suitable as indoor pets because their faeces make a considerable mess and cages are difficult to keep clean. Some hedgehogs settle easily into captivity; others remain restless and obviously distressed. Fleas may be removed using flea powder without harm to the hedgehog. Ticks can be pulled off with tweezers or smeared with olive oil to suffocate them.

Hedgehogs can be bred in captivity, though this is often unsuccessful. Mothers will eat new-born young if they are disturbed and abandoned babies are difficult to rear by hand unless they are already nearly weaned. Rearing baby hedgehogs requires patience, suitable food (not cow's milk) and constant warmth (over 20 C, 68 F). Most die, causing considerable distress to their keepers. Captive-reared hedgehogs can cope with being released into the wild.

Under the Wildlife and Countryside Act (1981), hedgehogs are granted a degree of legal protection. A licence is required to trap them, bringing British law into line with other parts of Europe. However, trapping is not a serious threat to hedgehogs over Britain as a whole and the law does nothing to protect the hedgehog from habitat loss, changes in farming methods or from the effects of agricultural and garden chemicals, all of which pose a far greater threat. By an unintended quirk in its wording, the Act also makes it illegal to catch hedgehogs using a torch unless a licence has been obtained first. However, it is unlikely that anyone would be prosecuted as a result unless their activities were demonstrably offensive for other reasons. Recent cases of deliberate cruelty to hedgehogs may result in legal protection being strengthened. The British Hedgehog Preservation Society was established in 1982 to promote the conservation and welfare of hedgehogs and to encourage education in wildlife matters.

In general hedgehogs seem to have established a fairly stable relationship with humans. They have been in existence for over ten million years, far longer than *Homo sapiens*. They have outlasted the woolly mammoth and the sabretoothed tiger and, despite being among the most ancient mammals alive today, seem well able to survive in our modern, man-dominated world.

Further Reading

Burton, M. *The Hedgehog*. André Deutsch, 1969. Reprinted as a Corgi 'Survival' paperback. Now out of print but often available through local libraries.

Corbet, G. B., and Harris S. *The Handbook of British Mammals*. Third edition. Blackwells, 1991. The definitive source book on British mammals.

Herter, K. *Hedgehogs*. Phoenix House, 1969. Now out of print but often available through local libraries.

Morris, P. *Hedgehogs*. Whittet Books, 1983. Written for a general readership and including informative and amusing illustrations by Guy Troughton.

Stocker, L. *The Complete Hedgehog*. Chatto, 1987. Particularly concerned with caring for sick hedgehogs at the 'Hedgehog Hospital' in Aylesbury.

Various leaflets, books, hedgehog toys and other items are available from the British Hedgehog Preservation Society, Knowbury House, Knowbury, Shropshire. Special hedgehog nest boxes are available from Garden Wildlife Products, 15 Malvern Buildings, Fairfield Park, Bath, Avon.

Further information on hedgehogs and other mammals is available from the Mammal Society Conservation Officer, Zoology Dept, Woodland Road, Bristol, Avon BS8 1UG.

ACKNOWLEDGEMENTS

Photographs are by the author. Line drawings are by Guy Troughton except for figure 1, which is by S. Wroot.